King

Pat Kinevane

G000149906

methuen | drama

LONDON • NEW YORK • OXFORD • NEW DELHI • SYDNEY

METHUEN DRAMA
Bloomsbury Publishing Plc
50 Bedford Square, London, WC1B 3DP, UK
1385 Broadway, New York, NY 10018, USA
29 Earlsfort Terrace, Dublin 2, Ireland

BLOOMSBURY, METHUEN DRAMA and the Methuen
Drama logo are trademarks of Bloomsbury Publishing Plc

First published in Great Britain 2023

Cover design: Publicis Dublin

Cover image © Leo Byrne

A catalogue record for this book is available from the British Library.

A catalog record for this title is available from the Library of Congress.

ISBN: PB: 978-1-3503-6879-8
ePDF: 978-1-3503-6881-1
eBook: 978-1-3503-6880-4

Series: Modern Plays

Typeset by Mark Heslington Ltd, Scarborough, North Yorkshire
Printed and bound in Great Britain

To find out more about our authors and books visit
www.bloomsbury.com and sign up for our newsletters.

ABOUT FISHAMBLE

Fishamble is an Irish theatre company that discovers, develops and produces new plays of national importance with a global reach. It has toured its productions to audiences throughout Ireland, and to 19 other countries. It champions the role of the playwright, typically supporting over 50% of the writers of all new plays produced on the island of Ireland each year. Fishamble has received many awards in Ireland and internationally, including an Olivier Award.

'the much-loved Fishamble [is] a global brand
with international theatrical presence . . .
an unswerving force for new writing' **Irish Times**

'Ireland's leading new writing company' **The Stage**

'the respected Dublin company . . . forward-thinking Fishamble'
New York Times

'excellent Fishamble . . . Ireland's terrific Fishamble' **Guardian**

'when Fishamble is [in New York], you've got to go'
Time Out New York

'that great Irish new writing company, Fishamble'
Lyn Gardner, Stage Door

'Fishamble puts electricity into the National grid of dreams'
Sebastian Barry

Fishamble Staff: Jim Culleton (Artistic Director & CEO), Eva Scanlan (Executive Director), Gavin Kostick (Literary Manager), Ronan Carey (Office & Production Coordinator), Freya Gillespie (Fundraising & Development Executive), Cally Shine (Associate Producer)

Fishamble Board: Peter Finnegan, John McGrane, Louise Molloy, Doireann Ní Bhriain (Chair), Ronan Nulty, John O'Donnell, Siobhan O'Leary (Vice Chair), Colleen Savage, John Tierney

Fishamble is funded by the Arts Council,
Dublin City Council, and Culture Ireland.

Fishamble's recent and current productions include:

- *Heaven* by Eugene O'Brien (2022–23) touring in Ireland and transfer Off-Broadway
- *Outrage* by Deirdre Kinahan (2022) touring and online, as part of the Decade of Centenaries
- *The Pride of Parnell Street* by Sebastian Barry (2007–11 and 2022) touring in Ireland and internationally, BBC Audio
- *The Treaty* by Colin Murphy (2021–22) in Ireland, Irish Embassy in London, and online as part of the Decade of Centenaries and Seoda Festival
- *Duck Duck Goose* by Caitríona Daly (2021–22) touring in Ireland, and online
- *On Blueberry Hill* by Sebastian Barry (2017–21) touring in Ireland, Europe, Off-Broadway, West End, Audible, and online
- *Before* by Pat Kinevane (since 2018) touring in Ireland, internationally, and online, as well as a bilingual version *Before/Sula*
- *Mustard* by Eva O'Connor (since 2020) on tour in Ireland, internationally, and online
- *On the Horizon* in association with Dirty Protest, by Shannon Yee, Hefin Robinson, Michael Patrick, Oisín Kearney, Samantha O'Rourke, Ciara Elizabeth Smyth, and Connor Allen (2021) online
- *Tiny Plays for a Brighter Future* by Niall Murphy, Signe Lury, and Eva-Jane Gaffney (2021) online
- *Embargo* by Deirdre Kinahan (2020) online during Dublin Theatre Festival
- *Tiny Plays 24/7* by Lora Hartin, Maria Popovic, Ciara Elizabeth Smyth, Caitríona Daly, Conor Hanratty, Julia Marks, Patrick O'Laoghaire, Eric O'Brien, Grace Lobo, and Ryan Murphy (2020) online
- *The Alternative* by Oisín Kearney and Michael Patrick (2019) on tour to Pavilion Theatre, Draíocht, Belltable, Everyman Theatre, Town Hall Theatre, and Lyric Theatre
- *Haughey|Gregory* by Colin Murphy (2018–19) in the Abbey Theatre, Mountjoy Prison, Dáil Éireann, Croke Park, and Larkin Community College, as well as on national tour
- *The Humours of Bandon* by Margaret McAuliffe (2017–19) touring in Ireland, UK, US, and Australia
- *Rathmines Road* by Deirdre Kinahan (2018) in coproduction with the Abbey Theatre

- *Drip Feed* by Karen Cogan (2018) in coproduction with Soho Theatre, touring in Ireland and UK
- *GPO 1818* by Colin Murphy (2018) to mark the bicentenary of the GPO
- *Maz and Bricks* by Eva O'Connor (2017–18) on national and international tour
- *Forgotten, Silent* and *Underneath* by Pat Kinevane (since 2007, 2011 and 2014, respectively) touring in Ireland, UK, Europe, US, Australia, New Zealand, and online
- *Charolais* by Noni Stapleton (2017) in New York
- *Inside the GPO* by Colin Murphy (2016) performed in the GPO during Easter
- *Tiny Plays for Ireland and America* by twenty-six writers (2016) at the Kennedy Center, Washington DC, and Irish Arts Center, New York, as part of *Ireland 100*
- *Mainstream* by Rosaleen McDonagh (2016) in coproduction with Project Arts Centre
- *Invitation to a Journey* by David Bolger, Deirdre Gribbin and Gavin Kostick (2016) in coproduction with CoisCeim, Crash Ensemble and Galway International Arts Festival
- *Little Thing, Big Thing* by Donal O'Kelly (2014–16) touring in Ireland, UK, Europe, US and Australia
- *Swing* by Steve Blount, Peter Daly, Gavin Kostick and Janet Moran (2014–16) touring in Ireland, UK, Europe, US, Australia and New Zealand
- *Bailed Out* by Colin Murphy (2015) on national tour
- *Spinning* by Deirdre Kinahan (2014) at Dublin Theatre Festival
- *The Wheelchair on My Face* by Sonya Kelly (2013–14) touring in Ireland, UK, Europe and US.

Fishamble wishes to thank the following Friends of Fishamble and Corporate Members for their invaluable support:

Alan & Rosemary Ashe, ATM Accounting Services, Mary Banotti, Tania Banotti, Doireann Ní Bhriain, Colette & Barry Breen, Sean Brett, John Butler, Elizabeth Carroll, Breda Cashe, Barry Cassidy, Maura Connolly, Finola Earley, John & Yvonne Healy, Alison Howard, Stephen Lambert, Damian Lane, Angus Laverty, Patrick Lonergan, Sheelagh Malin, John McGrane, Monica McInerney, Ger McNaughton, Anne McQuillan, Liz Morrin, Pat Moylan, Liz Nugent, Ronan Nulty, Lisney, Siobhan O'Beirne, Tom O'Connor Consultant, Siobhan O'Leary, Muiris O'Reilly, Andrew & Delyth Parkes, Margaret Rogers, David & Veronica Rowe, Judy Regan, Jennifer Russell, Eileen Ryan, Colleen Savage, Brian Singleton, William J. Smith, and Mary Stephenson. Thank you also to all those who do not wish to be credited.

fishamble.com   facebook.com/fishamble   twitter.com/fishamble

Acknowledgements

Thanks to the following for their help with this production: David Parnell, Liz Meaney, Bea Kelleher, Katie Walsh, Hannah Gordis, and all at the Arts Council; Ray Yeates, Sinéad Connolly, and all at Dublin City Council Arts Office; Sharon Barry, Ciaran Walsh, Valerie Behan, and all at Culture Ireland; the Nasc Network; Nik Quaife; Morag Deyes, Tony Mills, Kirsty Somerville, and all at Dance Base; Ronan Nulty, James Kelleher, Karen Muckian, and all at Publicis Dublin; all at 3 Great Denmark Street; Muirne Bloomer; all those who have helped since this publication went to print.

Fishamble: The New Play Company presents

King

by Pat Kinevane

Cast

Luther	Pat Kinevane
Voice of Tango Instructor	José Miguel Jimenez
Voice of Indira	Hilda Fay

Creative Team

Director	Jim Culleton
Composer & Sound Designer	Denis Clohessy
Lighting Designer	Pius McGrath
Stylist	Catherine Condell
Elvis' Wardrobe	Mariad Whisker
Make Up	Zoe Clark
Dramaturg	Gavin Kostick
Choreographers	Kristina Chaloir and Julian Brigatti
Sound Design Assistant	Aoife Kavanagh

Production Team

Producers	Eva Scanlan and Cally Shine
Stage Manager	Steph Ryan
Production Coordinator	Ronan Carey
Marketing	Allie Whelan
PR	O'Doherty Communications

Musicians

Accordion	Ken Whelan
Double Bass	Malachy Robinson
Piano	Katerina Speranskaya
Violin/Fiddle	Courtney Cullen

The production runs for approximately 80 minutes, with no interval.

King was first produced by Fishamble: The New Play Company in 2023 on national and international tour.

This production was developed with the support of the Nasc Network Commission.

Biographies

Pat Kinevane is a native of Cobh, Co. Cork. He has worked as an actor in theatre, film, television and radio for thirty-four years. In 2016 Pat won a Laurence Olivier Award in London for his Outstanding Achievement as an Actor and a Writer. This prestigious award was shared with Fishamble and Jim Culleton who have been integral to the production and direction of Pat's four solo shows. As a writer he completed his first full length play *The Nun's Wood* in 1997 which won a BBC Stewart Parker Trust Award and was produced by Fishamble. Fishamble then produced his second play *The Plains of Enna* (Dublin Theatre Festival 1999). Pat wrote *The Death of Herod* for Mysteries 2000 at the SFX. In 2008 his piece *Evangeline Elsewhere* premiered in New York in the First Irish Festival.

Pat has been touring since 2006 with his four solo pieces *Forgotten* (Irish Times Theatre Award Nominee), *Silent* (Scotsman Fringe First, Herald Angel and Brighton Argus Angel Award), *Underneath* (Scotsman Fringe First and Adelaide Fringe Awards), and *Before* (Herald Archangel Award winner) all produced by Fishamble.

Pat is deeply thankful to Fishamble for all of their work and endless support.

Jim Culleton is the Artistic Director of Fishamble: The New Play Company, for which he has directed productions on tour throughout Ireland, UK, Europe, Australia, New Zealand, Canada and the US. His productions for Fishamble have won Olivier, The Stage, Scotsman Fringe First, and Irish Times Best Director awards. Jim has directed for the Abbey, the Gaiety, the Belgrade, 7:84 Scotland, Project, Amharclann de hÍde, Tinderbox, Passion Machine, the Ark, Second Age, Dundee Rep, CoisCéim/Crash Ensemble/GIAF, Frontline Defenders, Amnesty International, Little Museum of Dublin, Fighting Words, Scripts Festival, Dirty Protest, and Baptiste Programme. He has directed audio plays for Audible, BBC, RTÉ Radio 1, and RTÉ lyric fm. He has also directed for Vessel and APA (Australia), TNL (Canada), Solas Nua, Mosaic, and Kennedy Center (Washington DC), Odyssey (LA), Origin, Irish Arts Center, New Dramatists, Irish Rep, and 59E59 (New York), as well as for Trafalgar Theatre Productions in the West End, and IAC/Symphony Space on Broadway. Jim has taught for NYU, NUI, GSA, Uversity, the Lir, Villanova, Notre Dame, UM, UMD, JNU, and TCD.

Denis Clohessy has previously worked with Fishamble, including the productions *The Treaty*, *On Blueberry Hill*, *The Pride of Parnell Street*, *Silent*, *Underneath*, *Spinning*, *Mainstream* and *Strandline*. He has also produced work for theatre and dance with the Abbey Theatre, the Gate Theatre, Rough Magic, Brokentalkers, Junk Ensemble and many others. He won the Irish Times Theatre Award for Best Design Sound in 2019 for *The Alternative* (Fishamble), *In Our Veins* (Bitter Like A Lemon) and *The Examination* (Brokentalkers), and in 2011 for Rough Magic's *Sodome, My Love*. He was a nominee in 2015 for Brokentalkers/Junk Ensemble's *It Folds*, was an associate artist with the Abbey in 2008 and was a participant on Rough Magic's ADVANCE programme in 2012. His work in film and television includes the films *Older than Ireland* (Snack Box Films), *The Irish Pub* (Atom Films), *His and Hers* (Venom Film), *The Land of the Enlightened* (Savage Film), *In View* (Underground Cinema), *The Reluctant Revolutionary* (Underground Films) and the television series *Limits of Liberty* (South Wind Blows) performed by the RTÉ Concert Orchestra.

Pius McGrath is an actor and creative producer from Limerick. He is Co-Director of Honest Arts Production Company, having written and toured original work internationally since 2013. He performed his first one-man show *The Mid-knight Cowboy* at the United Solo Theatre Festival on Broadway in New York in 2013. His company Honest Arts won the Cutting Edge Artist Award in 2015 at the Toronto International Fringe Festival with the Irish Times Theatre Award-nominated show *Waiting in Line*. His most recent original theatre work is the play *PUNT*, a story of gambling culture in Ireland, which was developed with support from Fishamble's New Play Clinic. He most recently produced the outdoor promenade show *Waiting for Poirot* in 2022 at the People's Park in Limerick City in association with Lime Tree Theatre|Belltable. His recent TV and film work includes: *Foundation* for AppleTV+; *The Gates*, directed by Stephen Hall; *Gravedigger* by Púca Bán Films and *Stormtroopers III* with Cork Racing Productions. His recent Lighting Design work includes *The Bell Ringer* by Charlie McCarthy, *Twisted Tales* with Opera Workshop, and *The Celtic Con* with Limerick Youth Theatre.

Catherine Condell recently worked on *Silent*, *Underneath*, and *Before* by Pat Kinevane for Fishamble: The New Play Company, and *Payback!* by Maria McDermottroe and Marion O'Dwyer as part of *Show in a Bag*. Catherine has worked in the fashion industry for 35 years, initially as a display artist and then as fashion stylist and fashion show producer. She worked for the Brown Thomas group for over 20 years and produced the Supermodel Shows in 1996, 2000 and 2003. She has worked with Naomi Campbell, Christy Turlington, Helena Christensen, Yasmin Le Bon, Eva Herzigova and Erin O'Connor.

Tango Fiesta was created in 2008, and quickly established itself as the leading tango company in Dublin. Kristina Chaloir and Julian Brigatti have vast experience performing on national and international TV. They have danced on countless TV shows, including *The Late Late Show*, *The Morning Show*, *Don't Tell the Bride*, *The View* and *The Afternoon Show*.

They have also featured together in many films and music videos. Their most recent video was the proud winner of the best music video award at the International Dublin Film Festival. Their other tango videos have been watched by over 10 million people on YouTube alone.

As choreographers, they have worked worldwide with huge international companies such as Riverdance (*Heartbeat of Home*) and Tango Passion, as well as many national theatre companies such as Rough Magic and Fishamble. Kristina and Julian are passionate about sharing tango with as many people as possible, and expanding the tango community across the globe.

José Miguel Jimenez is a Chilean-Irish filmmaker, actor, director and video designer based in Dublin. He is a theatre graduate from Universidad de Chile and Trinity College Dublin, and recipient of an Arts Council Film Bursary Award in 2020. Work as video designer includes theatre, dance, and film work: *Hamnet* and *Beckett's Room* with Dead Centre; *Salò, Redubbed* by Dylan Tighe; with Liz Roche Company, the film version of *DEMOS* and video design for *Yes and Yes* which premiered in Philadelphia last year. Film credits include: collaborations with director Áine Stapleton on *Medicated Milk* and *Horrible Creature*, both about Lucia Joyce; DOP for *The House Fell* by Maeve Stone, *Éist Liom* and *Tar Anseo* by OneTwoOneTwo (Cork Film Fest). As director: *The Future Has Been Bad* (Best Documentary Short ISA Awards 2020), *See the Man* (Light Moves Festival: Outstanding Overall Work 2017, Best Documentary 4th International Film Festival of the Caribbean 2019, Nueva Esparta, Nominated for Best New Documentary Tempo Dokumentar, Sweden). Current work includes: his film

NIDO – mentored by Apichatpong Weeraseethakul – is among 50 awarded representation by PlayLab Films; video design for *All These Words* by Kellie Hughes at MOLI in Dublin, based on *The Unnamable* by Samuel Beckett.

Hilda Fay most recently filmed the role of Amy Kane alongside Ruth Wilson and Daryl McCormack in the TV series *The Woman in the Wall*, written by Joe Murtagh and directed by Harry Wootliff for the BBC and Showtime. Further recent credits include Edna O'Brien's new play, *Joyce's Women*, directed by Conall Morrison for the Abbey Theatre; and the role of Joan alongside Jimmy Smallhorne in the TV series *Northern Lights*, directed by Tom Hall and Ruth Meehan for Deadpan Pictures and Lionsgate. Other credits include: Justin Kurzel's screen adaptation of *Shantaram* for Apple TV and Anonymous Content; the part of Bessie Burgess in *The Plough and the Stars* directed by Sean Holmes for the Abbey Theatre and the Lyric Hammersmith; the part of Veronica in *The Snapper* directed by Róisín McBrinn for the Gate Theatre, Dublin; the role of Jo Landecker alongside Elliot Page in David Freyne's feature *The Cured;* and the role of Granny Flynn alongside Hazel Doupe, Lalor Roddy and Dara Devaney in *Float Like a Butterfly,* directed by Carmel Winters.

Eva Scanlan is the Executive Director at Fishamble: The New Play Company. Current and recent producing work includes: *Outrage* by Deirdre Kinahan; *The Treaty* by Colin Murphy and *Embargo* by Deirdre Kinahan, both as part of the Decade of Centenaries; *The Alternative* by Michael Patrick and Oisín Kearney; *On Blueberry Hill* by Sebastian Barry in the West End, Off-Broadway, and on Irish and international tour; Fishamble's award-winning plays by Pat Kinevane *Before, Silent, Underneath* and *Forgotten* on tour in Ireland and internationally; *The Humours of Bandon* by Margaret McAuliffe; *Maz and Bricks* by Eva O'Connor; *Inside the GPO* by Colin Murphy; *Tiny Plays for Ireland and America* at the Kennedy Center in Washington DC and the Irish Arts Center in New York; and *Swing* by Steve Blount, Peter Daly, Gavin Kostick and Janet Moran on tour in Ireland, the UK, and Australia. Eva produces *The 24 Hour Plays: Dublin* at the Abbey Theatre in Ireland (2012–present), in association with the 24 Hour Play Company, New York as a fundraiser for Dublin Youth Theatre. She has worked on *The 24 Hour Plays* on Broadway and *The 24 Hour Musicals* at the Gramercy Theatre in New York. Previously, she was Producer of terraNOVA Collective in New York (2012–15), where she produced *Underland* by Ally Collier; *terraNOVA Rx: Four Plays in Rep* at IRT Theater; the soloNOVA Arts Festival; the Groundworks New Play Series; *Woman of Leisure and Panic* (FringeNYC), *P.S. Jones and the Frozen City* by Rob Askins, among other projects. She has worked on events and conferences at the New School, the Park Avenue Armory, and Madison Square Garden.

Cally Shine has worked across the United States as an actor, teaching artist, company manager and creative producer. Born and raised in Seattle, WA, she holds a BA in Theatre and a Minor in Irish Studies from the University of Montana and a Graduate Diploma in Cultural Policy and Arts Management from University College Dublin. When not working with Fishamble, Cally is an Assistant Producer at Once Off Productions.

Gavin Kostick works with new writers for theatre through a variety of courses, script development workshops and award-winning schemes as Literary Manager at Fishamble. Gavin is also an award-winning playwright. His works have been produced nationally and internationally. Favourite works for Fishamble include *The Ash Fire*, *The Flesh Addict* and *The End of the Road*. Works for other companies include *This is What We Sang* for Kabosh, *Fight Night, The Games People Play* and *At the Ford* for RISE Productions and *Gym Swim Party* with Danielle Galligan in co-production with the O'Reilly Theatre. He wrote the libretto for the opera *The Alma Fetish* composed by Raymond Deane, performed at the National Concert Hall. As a performer he performed *Joseph Conrad's Heart of Darkness: Complete*, a six-hour show for Absolut Fringe, Dublin Theatre Festival and the London Festival of Literature at the Southbank. He has recently completed a new version of *The Odyssey,* supported by Kilkenny Arts Festival.

King

For Fionnuala Murphy with my Endless Gratitude x

&

*in loving memory of my remarkable Brother-in-Law
Walter Drake. This work is dedicated to you boy x*

The music of the tango begins. The house lights fade.

In the darkness we hear the deep voice of an older South American man.

'The Argentine Tango is a dance of seduction. And two bodies . . . become one.'

Lights up on a lake floor of royal purple. A man lies in a foetal position. He rises slowly and magnificently and dances alone.

'There is passion in this union. There is muted lust in the tension between. They walk, and glance, sweeping and dragging, feet caressing the floor – all guided by fingertips and palms in this beautiful Game of Seduction and Freedom. The Argentine Tango.'

Music out.

Snap to darkness. A phone rings. It is lit suddenly. A woman's voice, **Indira***, leaves a message on the voice machine.*

Indira Howya ya mental patient! I'm out havin' a fag. I am bleedin' gee-eyed already. Me feet are mangled from the heels. I left your tablets ready for collection, OK? Flossy is all excited – don't worry, she knows that you will see her after the set for a rosemantic drink with her OK oooooooHHHH. I know it's a big effort for ya but I am proud of you for trying! And I'm married I am actually married Waaaaaaaa! See ya at Ten ya hunk of burning love! (*Hangs up.*)

Snap general lights up and the man who danced enters. He slams an imaginary door. Bulb flash and sound. He is panting and exhausted but also elated at his escape – to the inside. He is dressed in a shirt and trousers. He carries shopping bags. The space is sparse and hosts a table, chair – an ironing board and iron – an electric kettle, a basin, a small square mirror, a throw, a mop and bucket, folders of papers and a neat CD player . . . and a general feeling of tidy emptiness. Oh, and all of these, and his costume . . . are the richest hue of purple!

Luther   Doesn't get any easier I swear. Like Sisyphus, pushin' that fuckin boulder up Patrick's Hill . . . forever . . . haaaa! The second I leave here the fists of me heart grabs the bars of me ribs and screams 'get back inside ya Langer!' It's a daily battle but I am not a victim . . . cos I keep joustin' thru the sweaty fear and near passin' out panic . . . Just the laughs and sneezes of people rubbin' off ya on footpaths and looks that I can't fathom and the loneliness of walkin' into a crowd. No confidence at all. If it wasn't for Dad I would probably rot here. He gets me out every day. And thank God for that. And thinkin' of the Tango gets me through. The steps. Next foot then . . . slide, and on to the next. Like Dad and his dancin' with the end. Poor Dad. I am a little ray of fuckin sunshine amn't I? Haaa! Ten past Eight . . . I better get ready.

Distracting sound outside so he goes to an imaginary window.

And c'mere . . . I am supposed to be the one with psychiatric issues!! The couple across the road – every evening at this time – look! Every Evening! Out comes the power washer blasting a lake of suds at the Lexus hybrid. He wears noise cancellers on his ears and the rest of us have to bear the fuckin bedlam. And!!! All day Saturday and Sunday his wife irons everything . . . socks, sheets, baskets of clothes, cushion covers and all the curtains, including the net wans. . . that's how I can clearly see her through the kitchen window. (*Points to the pile of folders.*) So now I find out that He works for Irish Water and She is a Local Addiction Councillor!!! And I am supposed to be the mad one on the street!

Light bulb flash.

He has caught his breath by now and slowly begins to unpack his groceries etc. As he does, a close-up male voice, **Pawdy***, whispers heavily and swiftly . . . as the lights dip for this.*

Pawdy   It's me here. July in the year of eighteen hundred and sixteen. Still here in West Cork in the deepest countryside. Normally July is teaming with dragonflies and darting swallows but this July is bitter and the sky is ebony.

Lights surge up to normal. The delivery is pedestrian and calm as he mops the floor.

Luther   I visit Dad every evening at half four till five. Half the days he doesn't remember. And I usually gallop there and back really really fast but once a week I does a detour for my essentials, my allowance from the Post Office and me Prescription from the Chemist. I jog as rapid as I can without seemin' like a lunatic. Can't look at people for long. But I can look at you no problem – whether you are imaginary or not . . . because I am home now safe and boss in me own castle. I don't be in contact with many people and all I have is a landline. Can't do mobile Phones or Facefuck . . .Tried it . . . AHHHHH . . . too much!!! Too many crazies and gowls givin out. And showin' off. 'These are the carrots I grew in my old wellingtons . . . OMG. Greenfingers. You like this Sardinian omelette I baked for lunch . . . hashtag . . . Watch out Great British Bake Off. Ah Fuck off! Oh and Throwback Thursdays!! 'Here's a picture of me taken when I was sixteen . . . wasn't I a total messbucket???' No you were fuckin' gorgeous and you know it and you're fishing for compliments now to make yourself feel better for havin' married that prick of a husband with his Edwardian gate lodge and your beautiful looks have been flushed down the shitter cos that alpha bastard has worn ya down and now you hate your life!!! And I thought I was mad! Don't trust it! Too intrusive. Privacy under attack.

Light bulb flash.

The lavender levels everything doesn't it?

Plays **Indira**'s *message again but this time at kitchen volume. He listens to it as he takes small boxes and bottles from a paper bag.*

Indira   Howya ya mental patient! I'm out havin' a fag. I am bleedin' gee-eyed already. Me feet are mangled from the heels. I left your tablets ready for collection, OK? Flossy is all excited – don't worry, she knows that you will see her after the set for a rosemantic drink with her OK ooooooooHHHH. I know it's a big effort for ya but I am proud of you for trying OK?! And I'm married I am actually married Waaaaaaaa! See ya at Ten ya hunk of burning love!! (*Hangs up.*)

Luther   That was Indira. She got married there at five o'clock. They're havin' the meal now, just the family. She had me prescription ready fair play to her. But she left them with the older pharmacy Lady – Annunciata – and she puttin' her rollers in behind the counter 'I'm all excited boy can't wait to see her dress' but I didn't tell her I'll be yodelin' at the reception later – pretended I can't go tonight and got Anadin from her for me thumpin' Migraine!!! 'A Migraine is a terrible cunt isn't it? Take six Anadin now boy and six more in two hours alrighhh!! And tell your Father I was askin for him.' Annunciata is grand but she's a banjo mouth twangin' with gossip and I don't want anyone to know that it's me up there for the half hour singing in me fringes and flares! I've been steady now for a long time on me dosage. Have me bad days but mostly level and happy. It's a miracle I recovered at all . . .

'For small creatures such as we, the vastness is bearable only through love.'

And I am delighted for Indira. She found a great man in Justin. He's real Cork City . . . and she's so howya common Dublin. She says to me two years back before they met,

'Seriously tinkin' of goin' lesbian – all men are lower than a snake's poxy belly. I'm gone off cock really. They shud all be chopped off at bert!!' She's lovely. So I am more than glad she found Justin. He's doin' great – Insurance Broker – and they are now Missus and Mister Justin Casey!!! Haaaa!

He picks up a can of shaving gel. He presses play on the CD. He sings the first few lines of 'If That Isn't Love' along to the backing track into the can.

He lets them in here on his intimate, almost whispered romancing!

I'm not nervous about the songs. But I am about me date
with Flossy. I met her with Indira last week for a cuppa. She
tossed her hair a lot! You just have to stay busy gettin' ready
and that will keep ya calm boy. Today is the tomorrow you
worried about yesterday, and all is well Mister. This is just
like my case file when I was in St. Kevin's thirty-five years
back! Imagine! Thirty patients, thirty folders . . . all in the
cabinet of the nurse's station. I used to sneak a peek at the
others' conditions and casenotes whenever I got a chance
– usually when the staff went for a piss. I had them timed to
the millisecond. I was in a ward with a fella that clubbed his
aunty to death with the leg of an occasional table, an ex-
priest who walked around like a duck, and a retired judge
who thought he was Dana holding his wig like this singing
'All Kinds of Everything'.

Music off.

Starts to set up a mirror and basin.

I hate my sink in there, too small for shaving. This and the
box bedroom are all I use to spare the heat. Dad was lost
today. Poor ould pet. At least he is gettin' the best of care
where he is – and he is like a glossy penny propped up in the
bed. And this mad ould fella there too – Tommy Turnoff I
calls him! I goes 'Hi Tommy Turnoff'. Then he goes nuts,
'Turn off that fuckin television turn off that RTE, turn it off
now before I put me chair through it . . . Why do they keep
talking about William and Kate and fuckin Harry and
Meghan and that nobber Charles and that ould horse
Camilla. I am not paying my licence fee to see their inbred
fuckin mugs turn it OFF!!!' I do be near pissin laughin' don't
I Dad? He cracks you up too doesn't he Dad? Haaaaa he
does. I love to see you laugh. Yer Majesty! But . . . he was lost
today.

Lights fade once more . . .

Pawdy   I always admire you a chara dhil. The way which you devote yourself to your dear Father. Keep that cherish going won't you? In 1798 my own loving Father was murdered Luther. I will not, I will not eat my tongue.

Lights up . . .

Luther   Do you hear him too? I hear that voice but rarely now. Times he possessed me some hundred times a day . . . a constant manic chatter and I had no control as to when and where he would arrive.

He rehearses the song again.

Music continues . . .

Dad's business long 'go – He had a hefty coal round all over East Cork, up the road in Carrigtwohill, Middleton, Shanagarry, Cloyne, and every Saturday from age twelve I'd help out handin' down the sacks to his shoulders. Dad in the lorry cab and me on the trailer behind on top of bags of turf and slack in droughts and gales. The paws and jaws of us both as black as anthracite. It was a lucrative round, farms and convents and two Star hotels – they all needed hot back boilers and parlour glows. He made enough to raise me, run his Chrysler, and pay for Mam's tiny waist frocks.

He dances a little here . . . but a very staccato tango . . . almost dreamlike.

Every Friday night they would step out Gleaming – at dinner dances and contests. Ye'd never think he handled filthy bags from the way he handled Mam – placed her in his fingers like a cut glass feather. Every Friday night prize filling the cabinet with silver and crystal. By way of the Argentine Tango – the only dance in the World where lovers or strangers can literally dance heartbeat to heartbeat.

He dances this tango with shades of Elvis performance until he stops the music.

But during the May 'til September, fires were scarce so his golf balls subsidised us. Our fox terrier was whizz clever and was trained to sniff out Dunlops or Titleist in the rough of the links and courses surroundin' the city. That dog was a rare goldmine. Dad easily sold 200 a week thanks to Paisley – yes after Ian – no way as vicious but could smell his moment in the sun!!

Refers to the folder of papers again.

See the Census Woman called two weeks ago in a big warm herringbone ponchothing! I was the last she called to on the cul de sac. Minute I saw her I thought she looked worn out. I left her at the door and I got my form to give her and next thing she's ringing the bell again and her head bobbin' and I says 'You OK Ma'am' and she looks at me sobbin' and then down. She was in a puddle . . . poor hen, her waters broke so I sat her on the trunk in the hall, called the nines and the cops took her off within ten minutes. But Poncholady left these behind. And de Poncho! I left a voice message on her department phone. No one gets back to me – meantime I'm flicking through a best seller!!

Lights dip for **Pawdy** . . .

Pawdy   In 1798 my own loving Father was murdered Luther. Never booed a goose in his life – until that brave June day. He rose from his hazel chair in the corner. He took his big pike from up the chimney . . . 'I have to strike a blow beside them,' says he 'beside the Munster Men to battle the invader British' and he charges out and across the bog but never made it to the Big Cross as his mouth was blasted open to each ear by a Yeoman red. They burnt my Mother and Sister alive in the Cottage.

Lights up . . .

Luther   My mother was a woman of very few words. She is gone ten year now. Just went, in that chair. Earlier that day she said something bizarre to me. 'Son. Everyone comes to Tango after a deep loss'.

The Fair Deal Crowd told me they don't cover Dad's hair, skin, teeth or nails. The home provides all those services, but at a cost. 170 a month extra! All I have is me disability payment, so I had to get money from somewhere. He was always so immaculate of himself but gets distressed if he's not spick and span. So year one I sold all the furniture. Year two I pawned the silverware and crystal. Year three sold all Mam's bejewelled gowns. Year four just in the nick I saw an ad on Supervalu's noticeboard. Male warm up singer needed. You sound like Neil Diamond, Sinatra, Rod Stewart or Other? Three Nights a week from nine till ten . . . Travel Paid. Good Rates. Ring Davy Black's Karaoke Shack. 087 lalala. It's eight minutes in a taxi! I gets dressed here and dropped back straight after. And nobody 'cept Davy knows who I am!!

He sets up the iron and board.

GrannyBeeBaw taught me to iron. She's the only grandparent I knew. The maddest beautifulest bitch in Munster . . . dem's her own words! And she loved loving us all. BeeBaw was born to love. She sweated love. She took in oxygen and breathed out Love! She was called BeeBaw cos she was hit by an Ambulance when Mam was young. It broke her legs bad and when she was let out of the hospital after a month she got a smack of another Ambulance in the carpark and the legs were snapped again. But she was plowhorse strong and was donkey stubborn when she decided to be. I arrived six hours after Dr. Martin King Junior was murdered in Memphis, 4th April 1968 – so she insisted that I be proudly named Luther. And I am! And I am not gonna iron the curtains don't worry!!

Ironing.

Me seven years old folding pillowcases. BeeBaw talking her history to me. 'The Blacks and the Irish have more than oppression in common Luther love. They both sang to grieve. Sang from their humiliated souls. Treated like animals with no rights, no dignity. Dr. Martin King and Mr.

James Connolly should be honoured forever for fighting for us to be free. The sacrifice they made for freedoms . . . The Irish free at last from the British terrorists that kept us all in chains Luther love and other poor tribes all over the Globe. From Barbados to Brisbane to Botswana. But now we Irish are Free, free to sing our freedom – you free to be the happiest little Irish boy and me Free to be the maddest beautifulest bitch in Munster!'

Prepares food.

Better take me meds. I used to be so embarrassed handin' me prescription to the chemist below. I always felt judged and blushed every time waiting. But then five years back, Indira started and when I handed her me prescription she clicked with me, one, because of our names – she's actually called after Mrs Gandhi the first Indian Woman President – and two because she is so down to earth honest. I was on allsorts of anti-psychotic drugs but she's always treated me as just normal. She had her own rough years growin' up in Dublin. She lost her only two brothers to heroin poor girl so that – that raw struggle has made her one of the most compassionate people I have had the pleasure to know . . . and befriend. The best craic and wants to set me up with her now husband's sister, Flossy Casey. That's the main reason she asked me to sing later . . . so as to impress Floss. Luther and Flossy. Luther and Flossy. K.I.N.G. K.I.N.G. Keep Ignoring Nasty Ghosts. K.I.N.G. . .

I am sick of being unhappy. I am sick of being alone. One chair. One toothbrush. One type of jam. One light switch . . . before sleep.

The music – a dance has begun. The older man's South American voice returns.

'The Argentine Tango has another style. It is called the Milonga.

This dance is the dance of the poor cowboys, the lonely gauchos, who frequented local brothels, using the dance for

introduction and seduction. The Milonga brings hope –
earthy hope – rugged and eventual joy.'

Luther *dances a full brutal dance. The poncho is a huge feature.*

Out of breath, he speaks . . .

Luther   There's another ould fella in the home with Dad.
'Divorced beheaded died.' Thinks he is Henry the Eighth
and he's real old Cork, Montenotte, and he's always dressed
up with the bedspread caped over him and the wastepaper
basket stuck up on his head. 'Divorced beheaded survived'
. . . and he always lookin' for Catrine!!! 'Dat shu? Dat shu
Catrine? Did ya see Catrine Howard did ya? That fucking
bitch had two affairs on me. You tell her I'm gone to sue the
Howard Hole off her and if I ever get hold of her I'll chop
the fucking head off her in the Tower by the Opera House.'
Poor ould bastard. 'Divorced beheaded died divorced
beheaded survived!' Nothin' worse than a snob, but a Cork
snob is the worst of all.

Lights low . . .

Pawdy   I don't understand the sky, the rusty charcoal sky.
No dry wood to burn, but hellish frost with no food has
starved my beloved wife and two children. I begged the
Landlord to help me, 'Have Mercy Sir, have pity Sir'. His
men ran me through his ornamental garden with lighted
torches scalding my body everywhere. I keep talking to
myself so I will not eat my tongue.

*Lights up . . . Food and tablets are had. He speaks calmly and matter
of factly . . .*

Luther   At age ten I was puzzled. They'd practice the
dances in the front room with the record player. I'd listen
from the hall. The LP was all Tango music and started with a
man's deep voice. But never voices from their bedroom, no
sudden laughter, never caught them kissin', or ever touching
each other. That only happened on the dancefloor. Secretly,
she never stopped loving Mr. Savage. Secretly she was

dancing with him, and not Daddy. Dad was her freshwater stream. Safe. Savage would always be her salty battering Ocean. Back in a minute. Time for Imperial Leather!

He hits the CD player on and exits. The phone rings and goes to machine over the noise of the shower and him singing.

Indira   Maybe IIIIIII didn't love uuuuuuuuuu!!! Howya ya nutjob! Can't wait to see and hear ya!! Everything is ready and Justin I mean my Husbingddd . . . Has checked the Karaoke machine and all is sorted. I know this is a huge effort for you but I am so proud of you for trying. Flossy is all excited too. Oooooooh!! See ya soon ya loon!

He returns in a dressing gown. Barefoot. He turns off the CD player.

Luther   BeeBaw was banjaxed. I was twelve. She was out of her skull on drugs in the end. Just beautifulest her and me in the big room above us and she spilt her deathbed guts . . . 'C'mere to me boy, Luther. Listen carefully now . . . Emily your Mother had a hellish time before she married your Dad. She went out with a fella from Donegal. Theodore Savage. He was a new teacher in town. But a controlling bastard. First time she brought him here, my gums felt it. And Emily denied it always. But he bullied her, and pucked her about. And the worst, the fuckin' worst . . . he'd give her the silent treatment . . . wouldn't contact her for days and she weepin' and missin' him. Calculated Mental Abuse. And she was forced to go for a walk with him on the eve of their weddin'. When she came home she went direct to bed. No kiss for me. I snook in later to check on her and she conked out – but her pilla was bloody by her ear. So next mornin' I asked her to fill the scuttle and when she did – I locked her in the coal shed. She screamed but it's not called a bunker for nathin'! "Teddy, help me Teddy, Teddy pleeease!!!" The bunker was safest for her then. I know cos I had locked meself in there many's the time from my own violent husband. No man or woman should have to suffer oppression Luther. It's your birthright to be free, my love.'

The phone rings again. He answers.

Hiya. Oh now, no sorry. To the Commodore Hotel Cobh ya. Ah c'mere you're early. Ya. I'm not ready. I ordered it for half nine. Today yeah at around three. It was the Girl took the book . . . OK, I'll see ya then. You won't let me down? Thank you. Half nine so!

He hangs up.

See the Elvis songs, I started when I was with Mildred. I got out of hospital at twenty-two and we met in Roches Stores' café. She was on the till. We used to go to a piano bar in Tivoli . . . put your name up and be called thing. And I'd sing to her cos I loved her, so much. I had no confidence up to that. She made me feel so good about myself. We got engaged after ten months. I was workin' steady and getting' my life on track. Then she found out about my time in St. Kevin's. And she never contacted me again. I never loved anyone again because I couldn't unlove her for decades.

Can I ask ya, honestly? How do ya – or is it possible to – fall out of love with someone you once loved so Ferociously.

Let me introduce you all to the boozehound couple in number five! He works for Bus Éireann and She runs an Elocution school in her fancy shed out the back! Politicians, kids, best man speeches . . . Her slogan is on the garden wall – 'Let us help you find the voice that you deserve!!' Oh she does really well. But she's a fuckin' liar! Look. Census. House built before 1919 . . . tick! . . . Lie! Detached . . . tick! . . . 'nuther Lie – Husband's occupation . . . Private Chauffeur! Big bus drivin' fuckin' lie! All so when her ancestors look her up she'll be more respectable and wealthier than she actually is!! Shur when we waked Mam years back, they both called, pissed, with wine and Him holdin' a bunch of tulips! He didn't open his gob but she thought she was makin' perfect sense. She kept handin' out her card and asking people 'May I shhhhupply your demaaand, may I, I would be priveellllgge to suuppie your demaaaand'. He dragged her out after she vomited into the sandwich toaster! And my Mother laid out in the parlour with tulips on top of her face!!!

No remorse from Savage. For batin' her. Blamed BeeBaw and hit the whiskey after school. Year later Dad courted and married Mam. Savage followed them everywhere ravin' 'Ye'll never find my loving again, Emily, I see ye together, there is no fuckin' passion atween yous, you'll never have our love ever again, ya stupid gurnin' wee bitch.' The killer blow was they had me. Savage disappeared from Cork altogether.

Arranges ironed shirt and trousers.

These are for after. Sorry now I'm tinkin' out loud and the belt, jocks, socks here and the shoes there and the shirt. All ready for the girl Flossy. Third time lucky Luther. Ah sure it could all end in tears. Like last week with Dad.

Music in. Opens an imaginary door. Manic running through the streets of his mind to the bedside of his father. Music out.

Sorry I'm late Dad, there were loads of people. You rest there and I'll catch me breath. Dad? What's wrong Man? Ah Dad don't. Don't be gettin' upset. Dad? Ah Dad calm now. What? Whisper it. Afraid? What, afraid of What? The Dark? Sure the nurse . . . when you're gonna what? When you'll be dyin' . . . ahhh Dad.

A long pause.

C'mere Dad. Ye know Annuncy Anadin . . . yeah . . . Davy Black's wife . . . She said she went to school with you . . . Yes Annunciata! She told me the other day that you were the most beautiful man anyone ever seen in Cobh, Ever . . . bar none! So now boy!! Ah Dad, don't get upset Horse . . . Christ I didn't mean to upset ya Dad!

His recorded voice whispers . . .

'For small creatures such as we, the vastness is bearable only through love.'

When I see him like that I thinks to meself . . . Luther, You are slap bang in the middle of a gift. You are still pumpin' blood – millions, billions have gone before you. What they wouldn't give to be still around. But you are here now so lucky to have survived till now to taste the random wonder here on the Planet now.

Big bulb flash.

Your time. Drink it up. Get drunk on the seconds, in this Place in space this whirling ball of fire and rain and sand and Salamanders and Goldfinches, Snow, Pyramids and laughing babies, infants starving on roasting rocks and Mothers wailing under a merciless Sun

Big bulb flash.

and the Lioness gorges the new-born Gazelle and the Moon shines on lovers and battling salmon and breasts and groins and every beating wing

Big bulb flash.

and bastard cops kneelin' on Black necks and Taoiseachs with no bank accounts and Kaisers and beggars want to last as long as they can . . . pleeeese, as long as we can. Your time, your turn, Slap. Bang.

Huge bulb flash.

Final year in school and it was my last chance. For Elizabeth. I had fancied her all through and I just had to do it. I started writing the Valentine card in the end of January. The front had a huge purple heart. February we got a new English Teacher. 'Girls and Boy Pupils, my name is Theodore Savage.' He did the rollcall. After my surname he didn't look at me for a week. I didn't tell Mam or Dad cos I wasn't s'posed to know. On the 14th he sent Elizabeth to the canteen for cutlery and plates. 'As a special treat on this day of love, there is a wee slice of Red Velvet cake for ye all, courtesy of my good and faithful wife.' Shit! I think he saw

me hide my card in me desk. Then, in the middle of spoutin'
Keats he went for the jugular!

'I saw pale Kings and Princes too – pale warriors death-pale
were they all. They cried La Belle Dame sans Merci hath
thee in thrall!' What's under de lid Luther? What do ye have
under the lid?

Nathin' Sir.

What?

Shakes head.

Did ya ate your tongue.

Shakes head.

Open it! Open the lid.

And I did.

He ripped the card open.

'Dear Elizabeth. I think you are a very pretty girl. I am a
quiet fella and would love to hold your hand. Each time I see
you I fall under your spell or something!' Ya thick son of a
fuckin grandmother witch. Your granny is a witch, granny is
a witch, ugly bitch I hope she's dead, your granny is a witch
. . . come on girls and boy pupils . . . la la la!!

The kids underscore the next piece . . .

Cake flyin' at me. And forks. A frenzy of forks. One in my
arm. One in my forehead. I lay on the floor. Dad had to
come and collect me in the Lorry and reported him to the
Principal. The day after, Paisley was shot dead. We couldn't
prove a thing and . . . never sat my exams or went to school
again. For years I was terrified of everyone and everything. I
started to hear a voice. Pawdy. An Ancestor maybe? He came
to me from the past, for help 'cos nobody was helping him
there. So, I explained that 1816, Pawdy, was known as the
Year without a Summer. There was a huge Volcanic
Eruption at the other side of the World and the ash filled the

skies over Indonesia and then travelled everywhere causing the blocking of the Sun.

During the following, he sticks sideburns to his face.

Then he asked me to . . .

Pawdy   Never forget Luther. Please never forget, and please forgive, but you must never forget. Because if you forget it could happen again. They treat us like filthy pigs. We are nothing now, we are nothing. Something awful is about to befall us. Oh Perfidious Albion. They want us to vanish. To have no Census. No record that we exist. And a bigger vanishing will happen soon, a bigger hunger, an atrocity cleansing of us all in the name of a King. Or a Famine Queen that sits on a zebra covered throne, the Empress that will crush Hindus, slice Aborigines and Maori to pieces, massacre anyone who gets in the way of Royal tea and conquesting cake. May the jewels on her crown burst into flames and destroy the carnage in her soul.

Luther *reveals his Elvis costume. Glorious. He gets into it.*

Luther   I was in St. Kevin's for years. And to this day, the treatment is not there. I would love to go chat to a counsellor but the list is years long. So I'm still pushin' that rock up that fuckin' hill.

Bulb flash.

I wonder how many actual pictures were ever taken of Elvis. What would the total be?

I need a dress rehearsal. Will ye be my crowd?

He presses play on the CD player.

He sings the whole of 'If That Isn't Love' . . . Triumphantly.

The phone rings. He answers.

Hello. Who is this? Oh hello Nurse. Yes this is Luther. I beg your pardon. OK. OK. I understand. In his Chair. Do you want . . . But can I come in to . . . OK. I understand. How

early in the morning . . . I'll be in first thing. OK. Sorry
Nurse . . . Can I. Can I ask you please. Yes, please . . . would
you, for me, would you, after this call. Would you please . . .
just . . . brush his beautiful hair.

Tango music in.

Luther *dances the tango without voiceover. The dance takes him to
the ground. He lies there.*

A phone message from **Indira***.*

Indira   You there Luther? Pick up the phone. I gave it an
hour but it's eleven now. I have to let the band on. I'm not
angry with ya OK. I'm . . . not. I'm just disappointed to be
honest. Flossy is too. That you let us down. I don't know why
. . . I know you're there. Luther!! . . . Oh Jesus Christ Elvis
will ya please pick up the phone!

Bulb flash and sound.

Snap darkness.

The end.

Methuen Drama Modern Plays

include

Bola Agbaje
Edward Albee
Ayad Akhtar
Jean Anouilh
John Arden
Peter Barnes
Sebastian Barry
Clare Barron
Alistair Beaton
Brendan Behan
Edward Bond
William Boyd
Bertolt Brecht
Howard Brenton
Amelia Bullmore
Anthony Burgess
Leo Butler
Jim Cartwright
Lolita Chakrabarti
Caryl Churchill
Lucinda Coxon
Tim Crouch
Shelagh Delaney
Ishy Din
Claire Dowie
David Edgar
David Eldridge
Dario Fo
Michael Frayn
John Godber
James Graham
David Greig
John Guare
Lauren Gunderson
Peter Handke
David Harrower
Jonathan Harvey
Robert Holman
David Ireland
Sarah Kane

Barrie Keeffe
Jasmine Lee-Jones
Anders Lustgarten
Duncan Macmillan
David Mamet
Patrick Marber
Martin McDonagh
Arthur Miller
Alistair McDowall
Tom Murphy
Phyllis Nagy
Anthony Neilson
Peter Nichols
Ben Okri
Joe Orton
Vinay Patel
Joe Penhall
Luigi Pirandello
Stephen Poliakoff
Lucy Prebble
Peter Quilter
Mark Ravenhill
Philip Ridley
Willy Russell
Jackie Sibblies Drury
Sam Shepard
Martin Sherman
Chris Shinn
Wole Soyinka
Simon Stephens
Kae Tempest
Anne Washburn
Laura Wade
Theatre Workshop
Timberlake Wertenbaker
Roy Williams
Snoo Wilson
Frances Ya-Chu Cowhig
Benjamin Zephaniah

Methuen Drama Contemporary Dramatists

include

John Arden (two volumes)
Arden & D'Arcy
Peter Barnes (three volumes)
Sebastian Barry
Mike Bartlett
Clare Barron
Brad Birch
Dermot Bolger
Edward Bond (ten volumes)
Howard Brenton (two volumes)
Leo Butler (two volumes)
Richard Cameron
Jim Cartwright
Caryl Churchill (two volumes)
Complicite
Sarah Daniels (two volumes)
Nick Darke
David Edgar (three volumes)
David Eldridge (two volumes)
Ben Elton
Per Olov Enquist
Dario Fo (two volumes)
Michael Frayn (four volumes)
John Godber (four volumes)
Paul Godfrey
James Graham (two volumes)
David Greig
John Guare
Lee Hall (two volumes)
Katori Hall
Peter Handke
Jonathan Harvey (two volumes)
Iain Heggie
Israel Horovitz
Declan Hughes
Terry Johnson (three volumes)
Sarah Kane
Barrie Keeffe
Bernard-Marie Koltès (two volumes)
Franz Xaver Kroetz
Kwame Kwei-Armah
David Lan
Bryony Lavery
Deborah Levy
Doug Lucie

Alistair MacDowall
Sabrina Mahfouz
David Mamet (six volumes)
Patrick Marber
Martin McDonagh
Duncan McLean
David Mercer (two volumes)
Anthony Minghella (two volumes)
Rory Mullarkey
Tom Murphy (six volumes)
Phyllis Nagy
Anthony Neilson (three volumes)
Peter Nichol (two volumes)
Philip Osment
Gary Owen
Louise Page
Stewart Parker (two volumes)
Joe Penhall (two volumes)
Stephen Poliakoff (three volumes)
David Rabe (two volumes)
Mark Ravenhill (three volumes)
Christina Reid
Philip Ridley (two volumes)
Willy Russell
Eric-Emmanuel Schmitt
Ntozake Shange
Sam Shepard (two volumes)
Martin Sherman (two volumes)
Christopher Shinn (two volumes)
Joshua Sobel
Wole Soyinka (two volumes)
Simon Stephens (five volumes)
Shelagh Stephenson
David Storey (three volumes)
C. P. Taylor
Sue Townsend
Judy Upton (two volumes)
Michel Vinaver (two volumes)
Arnold Wesker (two volumes)
Peter Whelan
Michael Wilcox
Roy Williams (four volumes)
David Williamson
Snoo Wilson (two volumes)
David Wood (two volumes)
Victoria Wood

Methuen Drama Student Editions

Alan Ayckbourn *Confusions* • **Mike Bartlett** *Earthquakes in London* • **Aphra Behn** *The Rover* • **Alice Birch** *Revolt. She Said. Revolt Again* • **Edward Bond** *Lear* • *Saved* • **Bertolt Brecht** *The Caucasian Chalk Circle* • *Fear and Misery in the Third Reich* • *The Good Person of Szechwan* • *Life of Galileo* • *Mother Courage and her Children* • *The Resistible Rise of Arturo Ui* • *The Threepenny Opera* • **Jon Brittain** *Rotterdam* • **Georg Büchner** *Woyzeck* • **Anton Chekhov** *The Cherry Orchard* • *The Seagull* • *Three Sisters* • *Uncle Vanya* • **Caryl Churchill** *Serious Money* • *Top Girls* • **Shelagh Delaney** *A Taste of Honey* • **Inua Ellams** *Barber Shop Chronicles* • **Euripides** *Elektra* • *Medea* • **Dario Fo** *Accidental Death of an Anarchist* • **Michael Frayn** *Copenhagen* • **John Galsworthy** *Strife* • **Nikolai Gogol** *The Government Inspector* • **Carlo Goldoni** *A Servant to Two Masters* • **James Graham** *This House* • **Tanika Gupta** *The Empress* • **Katori Hall** *The Mountaintop* • **Lorraine Hansberry** *A Raisin in the Sun* • **Robert Holman** *Across Oka* • **Henrik Ibsen** *A Doll's House* • *Ghosts* • *Hedda Gabler* • **Sarah Kane** *4.48 Psychosis* • *Blasted* • **Charlotte Keatley** *My Mother Said I Never Should* • **Dennis Kelly** *DNA* • **Bernard Kops** *Dreams of Anne Frank* • **Federico García Lorca** *Blood Wedding* • *Doña Rosita the Spinster* (bilingual edition) • *The House of Bernarda Alba* (bilingual edition) • *Yerma* (bilingual edition) • **David Mamet** *Glengarry Glen Ross* • *Oleanna* • **Patrick Marber** *Closer* • **John Marston** *The Malcontent* • **Martin McDonagh** *The Lieutenant of Inishmore* • *The Lonesome West* • *The Beauty Queen of Leenane* • *The Cripple of Inishmaan* • **Alistair McDowall** *Pomona* • **John McGrath** *The Cheviot, the Stag and the Black, Black Oil* • **Arthur Miller** *All My Sons* • *The Crucible* • *A View from the Bridge* • *Death of a Salesman* • *The Price* • *After the Fall* • *The Last Yankee* • *A Memory of Two Mondays* • *Broken Glass* • *Incident at Vichy* • *The American Clock* • *The Ride Down Mt. Morgan* • **Joe Orton** *Loot* • **Joe Penhall** *Blue/Orange* • **Luigi Pirandello** *Six Characters in Search of an Author* • **Lucy Prebble** *Enron* • **Mark Ravenhill** *Shopping and F***ing* • **Reginald Rose** *Twelve Angry Men* • **Willy Russell** *Blood Brothers* • *Educating Rita* • **Lemn Sissay** Benjamin Zephaniah's *Refugee Boy* • **Sophocles** *Antigone* • *Oedipus the King* • **Wole Soyinka** *Death and the King's Horseman* • **Simon Stephens** *Punk Rock* • *Pornography* • **Shelagh Stephenson** *The Memory of Water* • **August Strindberg** *Miss Julie* • **J. M. Synge** *The Playboy of the Western World* • **Kae Tempest** *Wasted* • **Theatre Workshop** *Oh What a Lovely War* • **Laura Wade** *Posh* • **Frank Wedekind** *Spring Awakening* • **Timberlake Wertenbaker** *Our Country's Good* • **Arnold Wesker** *The Merchant* • **Peter Whelan** *The Accrington Pals* • **Oscar Wilde** *The Importance of Being Earnest* • **Roy Williams** *Sing Yer Heart Out for the Lads* • **Tennessee Williams** *A Streetcar Named Desire* • *The Glass Menagerie* • *Cat on a Hot Tin Roof* • *Sweet Bird of Youth*

Methuen Drama World Classics

include

Jean Anouilh (two volumes)
John Arden (two volumes)
Brendan Behan
Aphra Behn
Bertolt Brecht (eight volumes)
Georg Büchner
Mikhail Bulgakov
Pedro Calderón
Karel Čapek
Peter Nichols (two volumes)
Anton Chekhov
Noël Coward (nine volumes)
Georges Feydeau (two volumes)
Eduardo De Filippo
Max Frisch (two volumes)
John Galsworthy
Nikolai Gogol (two volumes)
Maxim Gorky (two volumes)
Harley Granville Barker
(two volumes)
Victor Hugo
Henrik Ibsen (six volumes)

Alfred Jarry
Federico García Lorca
(three volumes)
Pierre Marivaux
Mustapha Matura
David Mercer
(two volumes)
Arthur Miller (six volumes)
Molière
Pierre de Musset
Joe Orton
A. W. Pinero
Luigi Pirandello
Terence Rattigan
W. Somerset Maugham
August Strindberg
(three volumes)
J. M. Synge
Ramón del Valle-Inclán
Frank Wedekind
Oscar Wilde
Tennessee Williams

Methuen Drama
Classical Greek Dramatists

Aeschylus Plays: One
(Persians, Seven Against Thebes, Suppliants,
Prometheus Bound)

Aeschylus Plays: Two
(Oresteia: Agamemnon, Libation-Bearers, Eumenides)

Aristophanes Plays: One
(Acharnians, Knights, Peace, Lysistrata)

Aristophanes Plays: Two
(Wasps, Clouds, Birds, Festival Time, Frogs)

Aristophanes & Menander: New Comedy
(Women in Power, Wealth, The Malcontent,
The Woman from Samos)

Euripides Plays: One
(Medea, The Phoenician Women, Bacchae)

Euripides Plays: Two
(Hecuba, The Women of Troy, Iphigeneia at Aulis, Cyclops)

Euripides Plays: Three
(Alkestis, Helen, Ion)

Euripides Plays: Four
(Elektra, Orestes, Iphigeneia in Tauris)

Euripides Plays: Five
(Andromache, Herakles' Children, Herakles)

Euripides Plays: Six
(Hippolytos, Suppliants, Rhesos)

Sophocles Plays: One
(Oedipus the King, Oedipus at Colonus, Antigone)

Sophocles Plays: Two
(Ajax, Women of Trachis, Electra, Philoctetes)

For a complete listing of
Methuen Drama titles, visit:
www.bloomsbury.com/drama

Follow us on Twitter and keep up to date
with our news and publications
@MethuenDrama